# Mythical Beasts

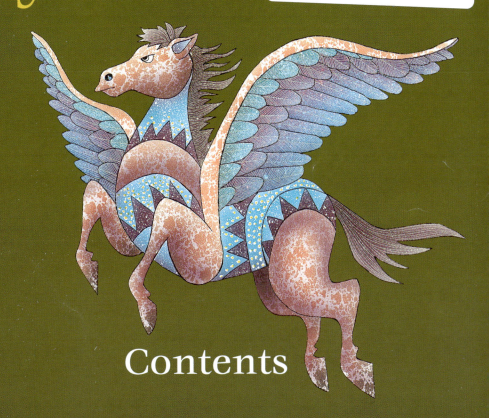

## Contents

| | |
|---|---|
| Mythical Beasts | 2 |
| Strange Footprints! | 10 |
| Mighty Tritonoclops | 14 |
| The Mystery of the Loch Ness Monster | 24 |

# Mythical Beasts

Written by Sandra Iversen
Illustrated by Jim Storey

Myths from long ago often tell us about strange beasts. Great stories of mythical beasts are told all around the world. Many stories of mythical beasts come from Ancient Greece.

## Cerberus

Cerberus (ser ber us) was a dog with three heads who guarded the gate to the underworld. Long ago some people thought that the dead went to the underworld. Cerberus wouldn't let the dead people out of the underworld and he wouldn't let people who were alive go in. One of the heads of Cerberus was always awake. It was very hard to get past him.

However, three people managed to get past Cerberus. The first person to get past Cerberus was Orpheus (or fee us). Orpheus played music to Cerberus and charmed him. Hercules was the second person to get past Cerberus. Hercules used his strength to get past Cerberus. The third person to get past Cerberus was Aeneas (in ee us) who went to the underworld to find his father. Aeneas carried a golden branch that had special powers to get past Cerberus.

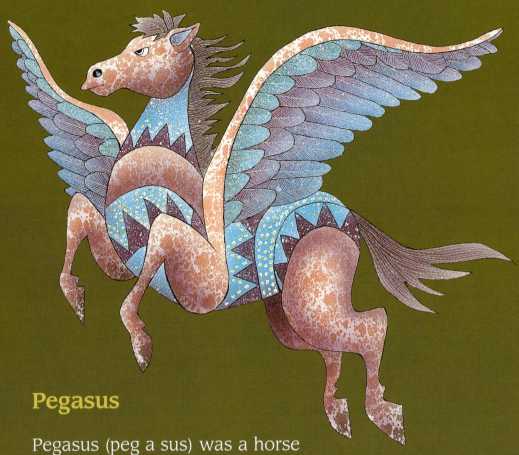

## Pegasus

Pegasus (peg a sus) was a horse
with wings. A brave soldier Bellerophon (bell er o fon)
wanted to tame Pegasus.
He wanted to have Pegasus for his horse.
Bellerophon thought that this would make him
very fast because his horse would fly as well as run.
Bellerophon used a golden bridle to help him
catch and tame Pegasus. Pegasus helped
Bellerophon win many battles until, one day,
Pegasus was stung by a fly. Bellerophon fell off
and was hurt. Pegasus never had another rider.

# Chimera

Chimera (kim ear a) was a fire-breathing monster with the head of a lion, the body of a goat, and the tail of a snake. The mountain Chimera lived on had land all around that was burnt and black from the fire of Chimera's breath. Chimera was very fierce, and the people who lived near were always in danger. Bellerophon and his horse Pegasus went to kill Chimera. Pegasus flew over Chimera, and Bellerophon shot Chimera with arrows.

# Griffin

Griffins (griff ins) were half eagle and half lion. They looked after gold and other treasures. Lots of other beasts wanted to steal the gold and treasure. The griffins were always fighting to keep the other beasts away. Griffins had a lot of courage and strength.

## Python

Python (pie thon) was a serpent that came out of the mud a long time ago. It guarded the land around Delphi (del fi). Apollo, the sun god, killed Python. The Pythian Games were started by Apollo because he wanted people to remember that he had killed Python.

# Centaur

The Centaurs (sen tors) were a tribe that were very fierce. Centaurs had the head of a man and a body that was part man and part horse. The most famous Centaur was Chiron (ki ron). Chiron was good and wise. He taught many of the Greek heroes about medicine and music and hunting. When Chiron died, he went up into the sky and became Sagittarius (saj it air e us), which is a constellation of stars.

## Phoenix

The Phoenix (fee nix) was a male bird that was bigger than an eagle. The Phoenix had very bright gold and red feathers. There was only ever one Phoenix at a time. Some people said that the Phoenix lived for 500 years. At the end of its life, the Phoenix would burn itself. A new Phoenix would rise up out of the ashes. Some people said that the Phoenix was like the sun. The sun dies in its flames each night and rises again in the morning.

# Strange Footprints!

Written by Sandra Iversen
Illustrated by Nicolas van Pallandt

For many years, climbers in the Himalaya mountains told of seeing very strange footprints in the snow. The climbers said that the footprints were very big and that they must have been made by the yeti. There are many stories about yeti living in these mountains. Some stories call the yeti the Abominable Snowman.

In 1951, a mountaineer named Eric Shipton took photos of very big footprints. He saw the footprints when he was climbing in the Himalayas. The footprints were too big to have been made by a person. The footprints did not look like animal footprints. He thought the footprints must have been made by a yeti.

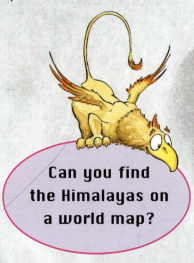

Can you find the Himalayas on a world map?

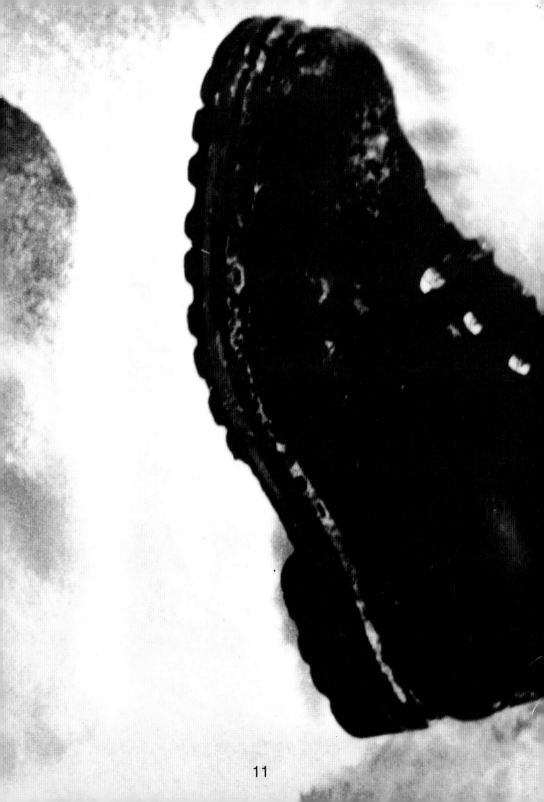

The Sherpa people have told stories about the yeti for a long time. The Sherpa people live in the foothills of the Himalayas. They say that there are two kinds of yeti. One kind of yeti is a huge animal that stands 10 feet (3 m) tall. This yeti is very fierce and is said to attack people and their animals. The Sherpa people say that once a yeti took a girl from one of their villages. They say that the other kind of yeti is a smaller animal that runs away when it sees people.

The Sherpa people say that both kinds of yeti are covered with hair. The yeti have longer hair on their heads than on the rest of their bodies. They have long ape-like arms, pointed heads, and huge hands and feet.

The yeti walk on two legs like people. They live in trees and often walk in the mountains. The Sherpa people say they have heard the yeti make a high-pitched noise.

Some people say that the yeti isn't real. They say that what people have seen could be big bears or apes. There are also some hermits who live alone in the Himalayas. It could be a hermit that the people think is a yeti.

If there are such things as yeti, how many are there? What do they eat? Why do they walk in the mountains? Why do they attack people? Maybe the people who are looking for the yeti will have the answers for us soon.

**Can you find out more about the Sherpa people?**

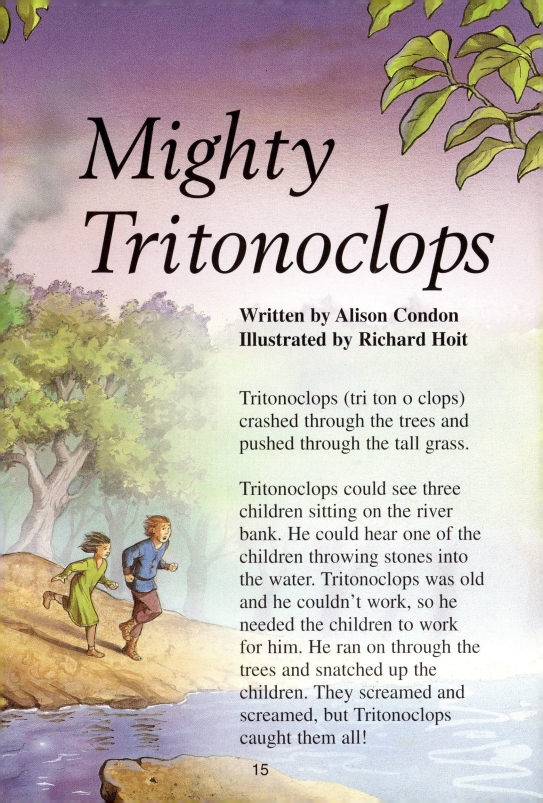

# Mighty Tritonoclops

**Written by Alison Condon
Illustrated by Richard Hoit**

Tritonoclops (tri ton o clops) crashed through the trees and pushed through the tall grass.

Tritonoclops could see three children sitting on the river bank. He could hear one of the children throwing stones into the water. Tritonoclops was old and he couldn't work, so he needed the children to work for him. He ran on through the trees and snatched up the children. They screamed and screamed, but Tritonoclops caught them all!

That night, the men in the village sat around the fire talking about Tritonoclops.

"Tritonoclops has come back," said Herlon, their leader. "I thought he had gone, because it has been many years since he has attacked our village. This time Tritonoclops must be stopped."

"But how?" asked his son Markon. "You are old. No one else knows the secret path to the cave of Tritonoclops."

The men talked all night. No one wanted to rescue the children. A boy named Starlin was sitting with the men. He stood up.

Starlin ran from the fire. "I will rescue my friends," he said. He ran through the forest until he came to a shining cave. A light glowed inside the cave.

"O Mighty One," Starlin called, "please help me save my friends from the terrible Tritonoclops."

"Very well," said the Mighty One. "You are brave, so I will give you two weapons. The silver sword can stop Tritonoclops. The white stone can kill Tritonoclops. But you can use only one weapon. I will show you the secret path to the cave."

Starlin followed the secret path until he got to the cave. He could see inside a room where Tritonoclops was sitting on an enormous chair. Starlin could see his three friends in the room. They were working.

As Starlin crept inside he fell over a stone. Tritonoclops heard the sound and looked up.

"Aha, another worker!" he cried. "Come here!"

Could you make a map of where all this is taking place?

As Starlin's friends ran to him, Tritonoclops blew flames over their heads.

"Not so fast, my workers," he said.

"I have come to rescue my friends," said Starlin.

But Tritonoclops just laughed.

"A boy!" he said, as he jumped forward. "How can a boy rescue his friends!"

But just then his foot caught on his chair and he fell to the ground.

Starlin stepped forward. In one hand he had the white stone and in the other hand he had the silver sword.

When Tritonoclops saw the stone and the sword he was very frightened.

"The Mighty One sent you," he said. "You will be too strong for me."

Starlin raised the silver sword and plunged it into the tail of Tritonoclops. Tritonoclops lay still.

Quickly Starlin and his friends ran away. They ran back through the forest, all the way to the shining cave.

"Good, Starlin. You rescued your friends, and Tritonoclops is not dead," said the Mighty One. "It is good that your village will be safe now."

# The Mystery of the Loch Ness Monster

Written by Tracey Reeder
Illustrated by Nicolas van Pallandt

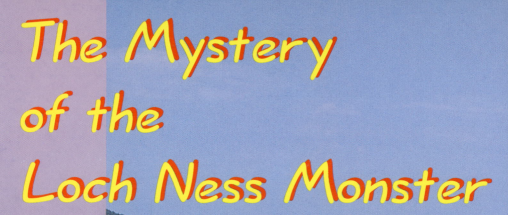

### Nessie

Hello, I'm the Loch Ness monster. Sometimes people call me Nessie. I live in a lake in Scotland. In Scotland, lakes are called lochs. The lake that I live in is called Loch Ness. Loch Ness is very long. It is 24 miles long (nearly 39 km). Loch Ness is very deep. It is nearly 1,000 feet deep (300 m). The water in the loch is very dark. This makes it easy for me to hide.

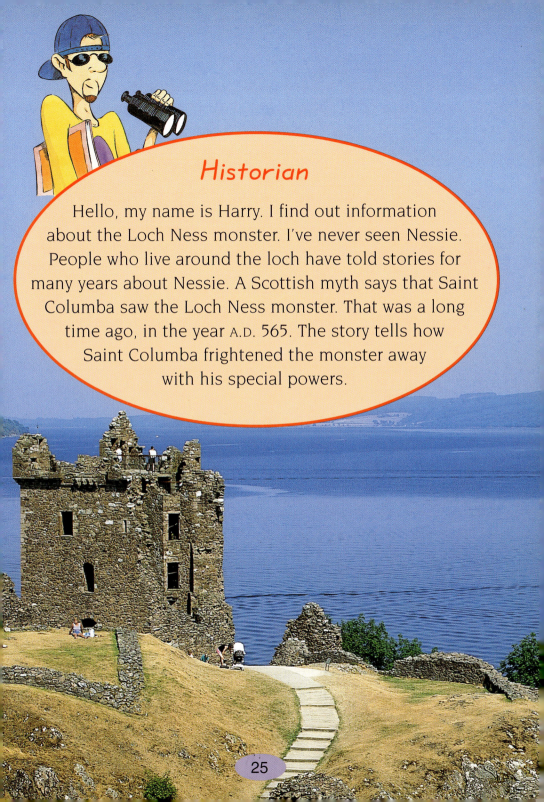

## Historian

Hello, my name is Harry. I find out information about the Loch Ness monster. I've never seen Nessie. People who live around the loch have told stories for many years about Nessie. A Scottish myth says that Saint Columba saw the Loch Ness monster. That was a long time ago, in the year A.D. 565. The story tells how Saint Columba frightened the monster away with his special powers.

# Nessie

Many people say I'm not real. But my family has lived in the loch for thousands of years. One man thought he had scared away my great-great-grandpa with his special powers. That man hadn't. My great-great-grandpa was just hiding.

Since then, we have been very careful and hide deep down in the loch. Sometimes I get tired of hiding, so I come up to the top to look round. I'm always careful not to get too close to people.

But in the 1930s, I became famous. One day, I was playing in the water. I was not being careful or looking out for people. I turned around, and I saw two people looking at me from their car on the side of the loch. I hid under the water, but it was too late. The people had already seen me.

After that, a lot more people came to the loch to try to see me. Then lots of people tried to take photos of me.

Now that I'm famous, I have to be more careful. I let people try to take photos of me, but I don't let them get too close.

## Historian

Many people say they have seen the Loch Ness monster. But scientists say there is no proof that the monster is there. Lots of people have been trying to find proof by taking photos.

In 1934, a man named Robert Wilson said he had seen the Loch Ness monster. He had a photo to prove it. The photo was famous for many years. Two men, Alastair Boyd and David Martin, found out the photo was a fake. Another man named Christian Spurling had made a model of the monster. He used a toy submarine with a handmade model on the top. Christian Spurling's stepfather took the model to Loch Ness where the photo was taken.

**What is a fake photo? Do you know an easy way to make a fake photo today?**

### Historian

In 1960, a man named Tim Dinsdale took a short film of what could be the monster. He couldn't get close enough for the film to show the monster clearly. He sent the film away to a special group of people who looked closely at the film. They said it was something that could be from 30 feet (nearly 10 m) to 92 feet (28 m) long!

### Nessie

The loch is getting very busy now. There are always lots of people around the sides of the loch. People come onto the loch in boats. Once, I even saw people in boats under the water! They had special equipment. I think they were trying to find me. I made some funny sounds, but I didn't let them see me. Some people come to visit the loch and stay for many years.

### Historian

In the 1960s and 1970s, people searched for the Loch Ness monster under the water. They used special equipment to bounce sound waves off objects. The special equipment is called sonar. Sonar "found" many objects. The people also used submarines to search the loch. Scientists from the American Academy of Applied Sciences took photographs under the water in 1972 and 1975. The things in the photographs were hard to see.

# Nessie

One day I was swimming around the loch. I looked up and saw lots of boats. The boats were slowly moving along in a line. I swam down to the bottom to try to hide.

I enjoy hiding. Sometimes I let people see me for a short time. I think one day I might let the people see me for a while longer.

What do you believe?
Is there a Loch Ness monster or not?

## Historian

Lots of boats were brought to the loch. The monster hunters called it Operation Deepscan. The boats had special sonar equipment to look at the bottom of the loch. The boats went across the lake in a line. The boats took two days to cross the lake! The special equipment showed some very big things in the loch. The things they saw were bigger than sharks but smaller than whales. But the scientists could not tell what they were.

People will come to the loch to search for the Loch Ness monster for years to come. One day, someone might find proof that Nessie really does exist.

# Glossary

- **constellation** – a group of stars that often looks like things they are named after

- **Himalayas** – a group of very high mountains found in Asia

- **loch** – a word (from Scotland) for lake

- **mythical beasts** – imaginary animals from made-up stories told throughout the years

- **Scotland** – a country north of England

- **Sherpa people** – a group of people (known as good mountaineers) who live in the Himalayas in Nepal

- **underworld** – a place beneath the earth where people were believed to live on

- **village** – a small town in the country

- **weapon** – anything that can be used for fighting (in both attack and defence)